SCHIRMER'S LIBRARY
OF MUSICAL CLASSICS

Vol. 2068

WOLFGANG AMADEUS MOZART

Sonata in E Minor
K. 304

For Violin and Piano

2 Allegro
10 Tempo di Menuetto

Edited by Henri Schradieck

ISBN-13: 978-1-4234-2706-3

G. SCHIRMER, Inc.

DISTRIBUTED BY
HAL•LEONARD®
CORPORATION
7777 W. BLUEMOUND RD. P.O. BOX 13819 MILWAUKEE, WI 53213

Sonata in E minor

K. 304

Edited by Henri Schradieck

Wolfgang Amadeus Mozart
(1756-1791)

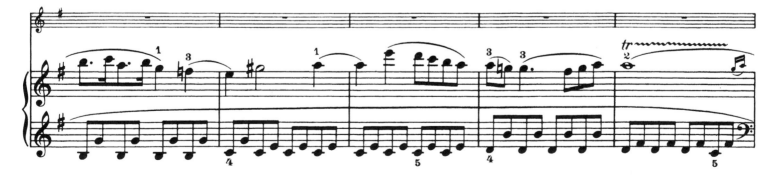

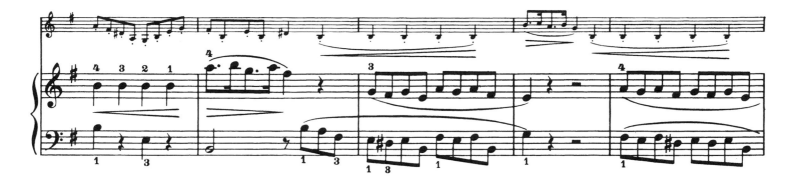

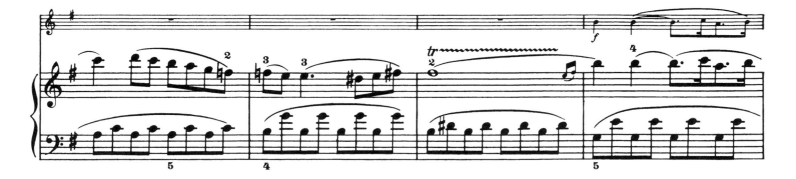

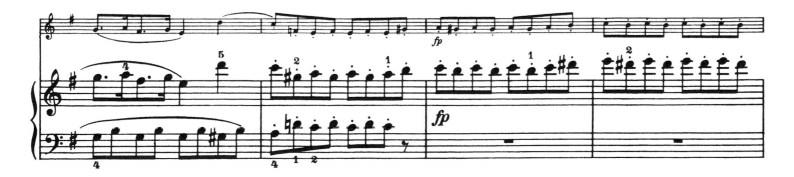

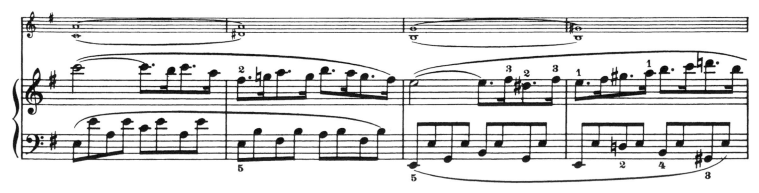

Violin

SCHIRMER'S LIBRARY
OF MUSICAL CLASSICS

Vol. 2068

WOLFGANG AMADEUS MOZART

Sonata in E Minor
K. 304

For Violin and Piano

4 Allegro
6 Tempo di Menuetto

Edited by Henri Schradieck

ISBN-13: 978-1-4234-2706-3

G. SCHIRMER, Inc.

DISTRIBUTED BY
HAL•LEONARD®
CORPORATION
7777 W. BLUEMOUND RD. P.O. BOX 13819 MILWAUKEE, WI 53213

ABOUT THE SONATA

Sonata in E Minor, K. 304
(alternatively K. 300c in the 1964 Köchel revision)

During a long journey of several months, Mozart composed six sonatas for violin and piano in the first half of 1778, of which the sonata K. 304 is one. Composed in Paris in June of that year, it has the distinction of being Mozart's only composition in the key of E minor. In a letter from Munich, Mozart's locale before heading to Mannheim then Paris, he wrote to his father, "I send my sister herewith six duets for clavicembalo and violin by [Joseph] Schuster, which I have often played here. They are not bad. If I stay on I shall write six myself in the same style, as they are very popular here." (Sets of six were a common publishing practice of the period.) These six violin and keyboard sonatas were published in Paris, dedicated to a patroness, Maria Elizabeth, Electress of the Palatinate; this set is sometimes called the "Palatinate Sonatas." Musically they are influenced by Schuster's music for violin and keyboard in form and approach, graceful and spare, using the violin as accompaniment to keyboard in some stretches. But they also reflect the Mannheim style of pronounced expressiveness. This sonata, K. 304, also has a French flavor to its second movement rondo melody.

No longer the star child prodigy, Mozart was a young man trying to make his way into a professional musical life. Mozart's father, Leopold, had traveled with him throughout childhood, but was unable to leave Salzburg. Instead, Mozart's mother accompanied him on this journey, which began in September, 1777 in Munich. After a long stay in Mannheim, an important musical center, they arrived in Paris near the end of March, 1778. Mozart soon found himself miserable there, his talents unappreciated. He sought important commissions and performances, but little came of his efforts. He also disliked the French music and culture of the period. His mother became ill in mid-June, possibly just before or during the composition of this sonata. She died in Paris on July 3 with Wolfgang at her side, far away from Leopold and their home in Salzburg.

Sonata in E minor
K. 304

Wolfgang Amadeus Mozart
(1756-1791)

Edited by Henri Schradieck

Violin

Violin

Violin

10

Tempo di Menuetto

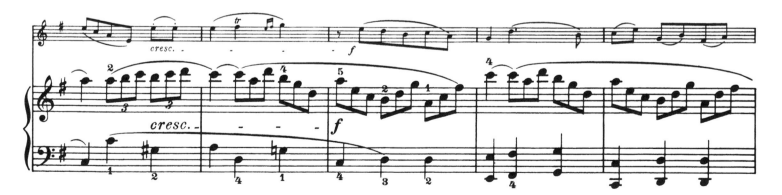

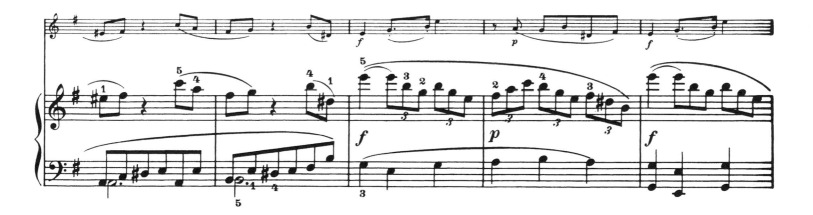